JESUS
IN THE
PSALMS

JESUS
IN THE
PSALMS

Bible Studies and Reflections to
Deepen Your Delight in Jesus

Maureen Shirley

ILLUMIFY
MEDIA.COM

Jesus in the Psalms

Published by
Illumify Media Global
www.IllumifyMedia.com
"Let's bring your book to life!"

Paperback ISBN: 978-1-959099-10-9

Typeset by Art Innovations (http://artinnovations.in/)
Cover design by Debbie Lewis

Printed in the United States of America

CONTENTS

PREFACE

Years ago during my annual Bible reading, I noticed that one of my study Bibles listed eighteen verses in Psalms prophesying the coming Messiah. From that point on, I always glanced at that section and read through the list, thinking it was pretty awesome. Around 2018, I began hearing the Lord instructing me to write a Bible study about Messianic prophesy in the book of Psalms. At first, all I could do was laugh. I repeatedly reminded God that I am *not* a writer. I know several published writers and would name each and every one of them, saying, "Trudy could do *this*. Tammy could do *that*. Joanne could write this Bible study for You very easily. But me? *I am not a writer.*" And so it went for several months.

Eventually, as you can see, I began to listen and obey my God. Since He was leading me through the writing process, most of it was very easy. Sometimes I strayed off of His path, which led to time-consuming delays and distractions where nothing was accomplished for long periods of time. Eventually, I would settle back into His way, and my path would be made straight before me.

During this journey, I came across a quote by Elisabeth Elliot, and it has been the first page in my notebook ever since. I could never open my notebook to work on this Bible study without seeing it, reading it, and being amazed and grateful for the gift God bestowed upon me: "This job has been given me to do. Therefore, it is a gift. Therefore, it is a privilege. Therefore, it is an offering I may make to God. Therefore, it is to be done gladly, if it is done for Him. Here, not somewhere else, I may learn God's way. In this job, not in some other, God looks for faithfulness."*

---

* Elisabeth Elliot quote, 2024 Goodreads, Inc., https://www.goodreads.com/quotes/168489-this-job-has-been-given-to-me-to-do-therefore.

I pray God has found this faithfulness in me and in this Bible study. I also pray that each and everyone of you find in this study what I have found. Knowing that all of these prophecies spoken of by David, the sons of Korah, Solomon, Asaph, and Ethan the Ezrahite in the book of Psalms have been fulfilled in Jesus Christ, the Messiah. Therefore we know we can rest in the assurance that every other prophecy, whether in the Old or New Testament, will someday be fulfilled by our Lord Jesus Christ.

I need to acknowledge the wonderful support from my family and friends in this endeavor. First of all, my husband John, who has supported me through the many ups and downs over the years. I especially owe much love and gratitude to the first editor who helped with this project, the late Pastor Paul Romig. He was instrumental in guiding me in the right direction and inspiring me to continue with the project when I was feeling defeated by the length of time this project required. He was an amazing man and author, and I'm looking forward to seeing him again where he is currently dancing on streets of gold.

I would like to mention by name my sisters in Christ, who dedicated themselves to eight weeks of working through this workbook in the summer of 2023. They each had good ideas, helpful insight, and positive observations that I believe put the finishing touches on this workbook. I am eternally grateful to each one of them for their time and commitment. I can never thank them enough for the blessing they have all been to me and for their continued prayer and support: Mrs. Becky Finger, Mrs. Eunice Docter, Mrs. Penny Ross, and Mrs. Kathy Moody, who has also spent untold hours contributing her technical support. Thank you, dear friends. I could never have gotten this far without you.

I also thank the entire body of Christ. The prayer support from countless friends around the country that are too numerous to mention, but you know who you are. You have all been such a blessing, and I have felt your prayers and good wishes all through this process.

I can't possibly express enough gratitude to everyone at Illumify Media Group. Their help and patience through every step of this process was incalculable. Thank you for bringing my book to life and helping me get it to the public!

He said to them, "This is what I told you while I was still with you: Everything must be fulfilled that is written about me in the Law of Moses, the Prophets and the Psalms."

—*Luke 24:44*

LESSON 1

PSALM 2:1–2

Why do the nations conspire and the peoples plot in vain? The kings of the earth take their stand and the rulers gather together against the LORD and against His Anointed One.

Please read the reference verse and the fulfillment verses below, then answer the questions on the following page.

REFERENCE

John 1:41: *The first thing Andrew did was to find his brother Simon and tell him, "We have found the Messiah" (that is, the Christ).*

FULFILLMENTS

Matthew 12:14: *But the Pharisees went out and plotted how they might kill Jesus.*

Matthew 26:3–5: *Then the chief priests and the elders of the people assembled in the palace of the high priest, whose name was Caiaphas, and they plotted to arrest Jesus in some sly way and kill him. "But not during the feast," they said, "or there mayt be a riot among the people."*

Matthew 26:47–48: *While he was still speaking, Judas, one of the Twelve, arrived. With him was a large crowd armed with swords and clubs, sent from the chief priests and the elders of the people. Now the betrayer had arranged a signal with them: "The one I kiss is the man; arrest him."*

Luke 23:11–12: *Then Herod and his soldiers ridiculed and mocked him. Dressing him in an elegant robe, they sent him back to Pilate. That day Herod and Pilate became friends—before this they had been enemies.*

Psalm 2:1–2 Questions

Why do the "nations" conspire? Is it because of fear, envy, or Satan?

What nations conspired during that time? What nations conspire today?

Name the people who conspired back then? Who are the people conspiring now?

Read these verses and explain how they illustrate FEAR of the Messiah.

Matthew 2:3–15

Matthew 12:13–14

Matthew 27:19

Luke 23:1–12

John 9:18–23

John 19:8

Read these verses and explain how they illustrate ENVY of the Messiah.

Matthew 12:13–14

Matthew 17:14–20

Mark 15:9–10

Do any other Scriptures come to mind to demonstrate fear or envy of the Messiah? If so, would you share them here?

PSALM 2:7

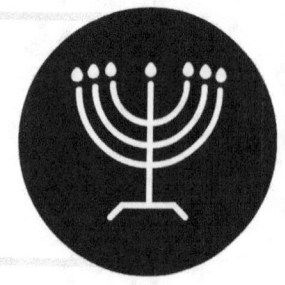

I will proclaim the decree of the LORD: He said to me,
"You are my Son, today I have become your Father."

Please read the following references and the fulfillment verse below, then answer the questions on the following page.

REFERENCES

Matthew 3:16–17: *As soon as Jesus was baptized, he went up out of the water. At that moment heaven was opened, and he saw the Spirit of God descending like a dove and lighting on him. And a voice from heaven said, "This is my Son, whom I love; with him I am well pleased."*

Acts 13:32–33: *We tell you the good news: What God promised our fathers he has fulfilled for us, their children, by raising up Jesus. As it is written in the second Psalm; "You are my Son; today I have become your Father."*

FULFILLMENT

Hebrews 1:5–6: *For to which of the angels did God ever say, "You are my Son; today I have become your Father"? Or again, "I will be his Father, and he will be my Son"? And again, when God brings his firstborn into the world, he says, "Let all God's angels worship him."*

Psalm 2:7 Questions

Jesus is the only begotten Son, the heir of all things. His kingdom was not established by a sudden resolve or after trial and error, as in an experiment. It was an eternal decree given by the Father Himself.

Can you find Scripture references to prove that Jesus was qualified to act for the Father?

Read Acts 13:32–33, then write out the promise. Is the same promise given to us when we are reborn? Do you rely on that promise? If so, why?

How do you think this promise applies to you?

Psalm 8:6–8

You made him ruler over the works of your hands; you put everything under his feet: all flocks and herds, and the beasts of the field, the birds of the air, and the fish of the sea, all that swim the paths of the seas.

Please read the following references and fulfillment verse for Psalm 8:6–8, then answer the questions on the following page.

REFERENCES

Genesis 1:28: *God blessed them and said to them, "Be fruitful and increase in number, fill the earth and subdue it. Rule over the fish of the sea and the birds of the air and over every living creature that moves on the ground."*

Ephesians 1:22–23: *And God placed all things under his feet and appointed him to be head over everything for the church, which is his body, the fullness of him who fills everything in every way.*

FULFILLMENT

Hebrews 2:7–8: *You made him a little lower than the angels; you crowned him with glory and honor and put everything under his feet.*

Psalm 8:6–8 Questions

Please read Colossians 1:15–20.

Please read Hebrews 2:7–8.

What parallels do you see in these references?

What do they each reveal to you about God? About Jesus?

Please copy other related verses here that come to your mind, and share them with the class.

PSALM 16:8–10

"I have set the LORD always before me. Because he is at my right
hand, I will not be shaken. Therefore my heart is glad and my
tongue rejoices; my body also will rest secure, because you will
not abandon me to the grave, nor will you
let your Holy One see decay.

Please read the following references and the fulfillment verses for Psalm
16:8–10, then answer the questions on the following page.

REFERENCES

Psalm 73:24: *You guide me with your counsel, and afterward you will take me*
into glory.

Psalm 48:14: *For this God is our God for ever and ever; he will be our guide even*
to the end.

FULFILLMENTS

Luke 24:5–8: *In their fright the women bowed down with their faces to the ground,*
but the men said to them, "Why do you look for the living among the dead? He

is not here; he has risen! Remember how he told you, while he was still with you in Galilee: 'The Son of Man must be delivered into the hands of sinful men, be crucified and on the third day be raised again.'" Then they remembered his words.

John 20:13–17: *They asked her, "Woman, why are you crying?" "They have taken my Lord away," she said, "and I don't know where they have put him." At this, she turned around and saw Jesus standing there, but she did not realize that it was Jesus. "Woman," he said,why are you crying? Who is it you are looking for?" Thinking he was the gardener, she said, "Sir, if you have carried him away, tell me where you have put him, and I will get him." Jesus said to her, "Mary." She turned toward him and cried out in Aramaic, "Rabboni!" (which means Teacher). Jesus said, "Do not hold on to me, for I have not yet returned to the Father. Go instead to my brothers and tell them,' I am returning to my Father and your Father, to my God and your God."'*

Acts 13:37: *But the one whom God raised from the dead did not see decay.*

Psalm 16:8–10 Questions

Who wrote Psalm 16?

Psalm 16 is just one of David's many "songs." He was not talking about himself. Whose body was he talking about not seeing decay?

Read Acts 2:24–33.

David clearly trusted God to keep His oath (covenant) of always having one of His descendants on His throne. Do you trust God to keep His word (oath) to you?

Why do you trust God?

Read the following verses and identify the promises of God.

Deuteronomy 30

Titus 1:1–3

2 Peter 1:3–4

How have you seen evidence of God keeping His promises to you in your own life?

LESSON 2

PSALM 22:1

*My God, my God, why have you forsaken me? Why are you so far
from saving me, so far from the words of my groaning?*

Please read the references and fulfillment verses for Psalm 22. Then answer
the questions on the following page.

REFERENCES

2 Chronicles 15:2: *He went out to meet Asa and said to him, "Listen to me, Asa
and all Judah and Benjamin. The LORD is with you when you are with him. If
you seek him, he will be found by you, but if you forsake him, he will forsake you."*

Psalm 27:10: *Though my father and mother forsake me, the LORD will receive me.*

FULFILLMENT

Matthew 27:46: *About the ninth hour Jesus cried out in a loud voice, "Eli, Eli,
lama sabachthani?" which means, "My God, my God, why have you forsaken me?.*

Psalm 22:1 Questions

Psalm 22 is another example of King David writing as a prophet. This psalm was written many centuries before crucifixion was a commonly used form of punishment.

Have you ever felt abandoned by God? If so, what made you feel that way?

Have you ever felt forsaken by God?

Can God forsake you? Please explain.

Read 2 Chronicles 15:2: What does this Scripture tell you about being forsaken by God?

Read our fulfillment verse, Matthew 27:46. Why did Jesus feel forsaken by God when He and the Father were one?

Are there other examples in the Bible of Jesus calling his Father, "God"? Or calling God His "Father"?

PSALM 22:7–8

All who see me mock me; they hurl insults, shaking their heads:
"He trusts in the LORD; let the LORD rescue him. Let him deliver
him, since he delights in him."

Please read the reference verses below and the fulfilment verse for Psalm 22:7–8, then answer the questions on the following page.

REFERENCES

Galatians 6:7: *Do not be deceived: God cannot be mocked. A man reaps what he sows.*

John 1:44–46: *Philip, like Andrew and Peter, was from the town of Bethsaida. Philip found Nathanael and told him, "We have found the one Moses wrote about in the Law, and about whom the prophets also wrote—Jesus of Nazareth, the son of Joseph." "Nazareth! Can anything good come from there?" Nathanael asked. "Come and see," said Philip.*

FULFILLMENT

Matthew 27:39–40: *Those who passed by hurled insults at him, shaking their heads and saying, "You who are going to destroy the temple and build it in three days, save yourself! Come down from the cross, if you are the Son of God!"*

Psalm 22:7–8 Questions

Read Galatians 6:7. Can God be mocked without consequences? What could some of those consequences be?

Read John 1:44–46. Have you ever been stereotyped and mocked because of where you were from or how you looked ? How did it make you feel? To what degree do the negative words of others affect you?

Read John 2:19: *Jesus answered them, "Destroy this temple, and I will raise it again in three days."*

Read the fulfillment verses, Matthew 27:39–40. Were the accusers quoting Jesus accurately or distorting His words?

Read John 2:20–22. Was Jesus referring to the same temple as His accusers? Did His disciples realize it at the time?

Did Jesus allow the mocking to aggravate Him? Why or why not?

Key takeaway: Jesus knew who He was and to whom He belonged.

PSALM 22:15

*My strength is dried up like a potsherd, and my tongue sticks to
the roof of my mouth; you lay me in the dust of death.*

Please read the reference verses and fulfillment verse below for Psalm 22:15,
then answer the questions on the next page.

REFERENCES

Psalm 104:29: *When you hide your face, they are terrified; when you take away
their breath, they die and return to the dust.*

Job 34:14–15: *If it were his intention and he withdrew his spirit and breath, all
mankind would perish together and man would return to the dust.*

FULFILLMENT

John 19:28: *Later, knowing that all was now completed, and so that the Scripture
would be fulfilled, Jesus said, "I am thirsty."*

Psalm 22:15 Questions

Read Job 34:14–15.

God could easily take the breath from all of us and return us to the dust, but He chose not to. He sent His Son instead. What do you think keeps God from returning all of us to the dust right now?

Can you cite Scripture references to support God's choice?

Find the definition of *atonement* and write it below. Are there things in your life that you need to atone for or has that been done?

PSALM 22:16

Dogs* surround me; a band of evil men has encircled me;
they have pierced my hands and my feet.

Please read the reference verse below and the fulfilment verses, then answer the questions on the following page.

REFERENCE

Zechariah 12:10: *And I will pour out on the house of David and the inhabitants of Jerusalem a spirit of grace and supplication. They will look on me, the one they have pierced, and they will mourn for him as one mourns for an only child, and grieve bitterly for him as one grieves for a firstborn son.*

FULFILLMENTS

John 19:34: *Instead, one of the soldiers pierced Jesus' side with a spear, bringing a sudden flow of blood and water.*

John 19:37: *and, as another scripture says, "they will look on the one they have pierced."*

---

* A metaphor for *enemy*

Psalm 22:16 Questions

Please read John 19:33–34.

Historically, who pierced Jesus' side and why?

On the human, maybe brutal side, why did this person do it?

Scientifically, why did that prove Jesus was already dead?

Whose testimony was John speaking of?

Read Mark 15:44-45. Joseph of Arimathea knew that Jesus was dead and went to Pilate to ask for his body. Pilate did not know Jesus had died, so he asked for more evidence by calling the centurion. The centurion (also a man of experience) replied that it was so.

Who decided it was time for Jesus to die?

PSALM 22:18

They divide my garments among them
and cast lots for my clothing.

Please read the reference verses and the fulfillment verse below, then answer the questions on the following page.

REFERENCES

Matthew 27:35: *When they had crucified him, they divided up his clothes by casting lots.*

Mark 15:24: *And they crucified him. Dividing up his clothes, they cast lots to see what each would get.*

FULFILLMENT

John 19:23: *When the soldiers crucified Jesus, they took his clothes, dividing them into four shares, one for each of them, with the undergarment remaining. This garment was seamless, woven in one piece from top to bottom. "Let's not tear it," they said to one another. "Let's decide by lot who will get it." This happened that the scripture might be fulfilled which said, "They divided my garments among them and cast lots for my clothing."*

Psalm 22:18 Questions

When humiliated or disgraced, we all need to respond as David did by crying out to the Lord: "*But you, O LORD, be not far off; O my Strength, come quickly to help me*" (Psalm 22:19). Perhaps the greatest humiliation to any of us would be to be robbed of everything, even our clothing (this happened to the Holocaust victims as well). Most of us, thankfully, will never know that humiliation.

How do you react when you come face-to-face with an obvious homeless person? Do you feel compassion or contempt? Do you act? Is your action preplanned or case by case?

Do you feel compassion or contempt for someone you hear about who has had their sin publicly exposed? Do you sense their humiliation?

Have you ever had one of your sins brought into the light? If so, by whom? Was it a person or the Holy Spirit? Was it done in love, or out of revenge and betrayal?

PSALM 22:22

I will declare your name to my brothers;
in the congregation I will praise you.

Please read the reference verses and fulfillment verses below, then answer the questions on the following page.

REFERENCES

Matthew 11:25: *At that time Jesus said, "I will praise you, Father, Lord of heaven and earth, because you have hidden these things from the wise and learned, and revealed them to little children."*

John 5:19: *Jesus gave them this answer: "I tell you the truth, the Son can do nothing by himself; he can do only what he sees his Father doing, because whatever the Father does the Son also does."*

FULFILLMENTS

Luke 10:21: *At that time Jesus, full of joy through the Holy Spirit, said, "I praise you, Father, Lord of heaven and earth, because you have hidden these things from the wise and learned, and revealed them to little children. Yes, Father, for this was your good pleasure."*

Hebrews 2:11–12: *Both the one who makes men holy and those who are made holy are of the same family. So Jesus is not ashamed to call them brothers. He says, "I will declare your name to my brothers; in the presence of the congregation I will sing your praises."*

Psalm 22:22 Questions

Judah is the Hebrew word for *praised*. The tribe of Judah was always first in battle and in any conflict. Meaning, praise should always be at the forefront of any of our actions, thoughts, and prayers.

Read Matthew 12:25. Do you remember the last time you publicly praised Jesus? How did you do it? Did you say, "Praise Jesus!" or share a testimony?

When Jesus delivers us in our hour of need, it is usually done quietly. We need to thank Him and publicly acknowledge what He has done for us at every opportunity. Is that hard for you? Read Mark 8:38. What does Jesus say will happen if you are ashamed of Him?

Read John 5:19. Jesus fully acknowledges that He can do *nothing* without His Father.

Read John 7:16–18: *Jesus answered, "My teaching is not my own. It comes from him who sent me. If anyone chooses to do God's will, he will find out whether my teaching comes from God or whether I speak on my own. He who speaks on his own does so to gain honor for himself, but he who works for the honor of the one who sent him is a man of truth; there is nothing false about him."*

Read John 8:26–28: *"I have much to say in judgement of you. But he who sent me is reliable, and what I have heard from him I tell the world." They did not understand that he was telling them about his Father. So Jesus said, "When you have lifted up the Son of Man, then you will know that I am the one I claim to be and that I do nothing on my own but speak just what the Father has taught me."*

Read John 12:49–50: *For I did not speak of my own accord, but the Father who sent me commanded me what to say and how to say it. I know that his command leads to eternal life. So whatever I say is just what the Father has told me to say.*

If Jesus can do *nothing* without His Father, how can we expect to be successful in our lives, our ministries, our marriages, or in anything else if we do not ask for God's guidance in everything we do. Our success depends on Jesus living His life in and through us.

Do you depend on God or yourself when you are facing life decisions?

If God has guided you, do you publicly give Him praise?

Jesus died for our sins, knowing full well the horror and pain He would be facing. Should He be publicly praised for that?

LESSON 3

PSALM 31:5

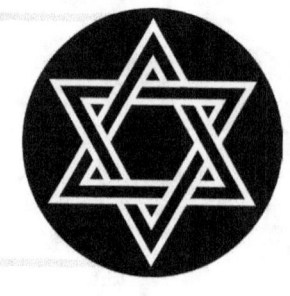

Into your hands I commit my spirit; redeem me,
O LORD, the God of truth.

Please read the reference verses and fulfillment verse below, then answer the questions on the next page.

REFERENCES

Matthew 27:50: *And when Jesus had cried out again in a loud voice, he gave up his spirit.*

John 19:30: *When he had received the drink, Jesus said, "It is finished." With that, he bowed his head and gave up his spirit.*

Acts 7:59–60: *While they were stoning him, Stephen prayed, "Lord Jesus, receive my spirit." Then he fell on his knees and cried out, "Lord, do not hold this sin against them." When he had said this, he fell asleep.*

1 Peter 2:23: *When they hurled their insults at him, he did not retaliate; when he suffered, he made no threats. Instead, he entrusted himself to him who judges justly.*

FULFILLMENT

Luke 23:46: *Jesus called out with a loud voice, "Father, into your hands I commit my spirit."*

Psalm 31:5 Questions

Read Acts 7:59–60. While Stephen was being stoned, what did he do?

Are you willing to fully give yourself over to God? Are you willing to forgive the people who have wronged you the most? Are you willing to forgive those who have betrayed you? Would you give your life to God? Would you die for God?

Do you find yourself giving God the most difficult things to handle while depending on yourself for the easier things?

Can you freely pass on the good gifts from God to others? His love, grace, and mercy are endless to us. Do you routinely give the same to others?

Read Romans 12:1. What is Paul asking us to do for God?

PSALM 34:19–20

"A righteous man may have many troubles,
*but the L*ORD *delivers him from them all;*
he protects all his bones, not one of them will be broken.

Please read the following reference verse and fulfillment verse, then answer the questions on the following page.

REFERENCE

Proverbs 24:16: *For though a righteous man falls seven times, he rises again.*

FULFILLMENT:

John 19:36: *These things happened so that the scripture would be fulfilled: "Not one of his bones will be broken."*

(David was also pleading for Gods protection in times of crisis.)

Psalm 34:19–20 Questions

We all will fall many times, but the Lord will always lift us back up because we are righteous. We have been given the righteousness of Christ; therefore we are righteous.

Cite some verses that show God's willingness to continue to pick us up when we fall.

Psalm 5:12:For *surely, O LORD, you bless the righteous; you surround them with your favor as with a shield.*

Psalm 71:2: *"Rescue me and deliver me in your righteousness; turn your ear to me and save me.*

Romans 3:23–24: *For all have sinned and fall short of the glory of God, and are justified freely by his grace through the redemption that came by Christ Jesus.*

Have there been specific times in your life that you can look back on and know God was there to pick you up? Did you even realize you needed Him at the time?

Have you ever tried to do it all on your own? If yes, were you successful? Can you explain the circumstances?

PSALM 35:11

Ruthless witnesses come forward;
they question me on things I know nothing about.

Please read the following reference verse and fulfillment verse, then answer the questions on the following page.

REFERENCES

Matthew 26:59–60: *The chief priests and the whole Sanhedrin were looking for false evidence against Jesus so that they could put him to death. But they did not find any, though many false witnesses came forward.*

Acts 6:12–14: *So they stirred up the people and the elders and the teachers of the law. They seized Stephen and brought him before the Sanhedrin. They produced false witnesses, who testified, "This fellow never stops speaking against this holy place and against the law. For we have heard him say that this Jesus of Nazareth will destroy this place and change the customs Moses handed down to us."*

FULFILLMENT

Mark 14:57–59: *Then some stood up and gave this false testimony against him: "We heard him say, 'I will destroy this temple made with human hands and in three days will build another, not made with hands.'" Yet even then their testimony did not agree.*

They were looking for people who would distort some of Jesus' teachings.

Psalm 35:11 Questions

Read Matthew 26:59–60. Has anyone ever purposefully slandered you? Did they do it because you were a Christian? Were they also a Christian? What did they have to gain?

Has anyone ever looked for reasons to belittle you, humiliate you, or destroy you? Did you want to retaliate, get revenge, and give it back to them tenfold?

Why didn't Jesus retaliate or defend Himself to the Sanhedrin?

PSALM 35:19

"Let not those gloat over me
who are my enemies without cause;
let not those who hate me without reason maliciously
wink the eye.

Please read the following references and fulfillment verse, then answer the questions on the following page.

REFERENCES

Psalm 69:4: *Those who hate me without reason outnumber the hairs of my head.*

John 15:18: *If the world hates you, keep in mind that it hated me first.*

FULFILLMENT

John 15:25: *But this is to fulfill what is written in their Law: "They hated me without reason."*

Psalm 35:19 Questions

Why do you think so many people hated Jesus? Was it because of fear or lack of understanding? Were they jealous of Jesus? If so, why?

Can you cite some Scripture references to support your answer? (See Psalm 2:1–2 for fear, jealousy, and misunderstanding.)

Jesus spoke often about hate and how we should deal with it. Can you cite some Scripture references that deal with the issue of hate?

Does God hate? If so, what does the Bible say He hates?

Has God ever mentioned anyone specific whom He hates? Who comes to mind? Can you cite the Scripture?

Psalm 38:11

My friends and companions avoid me because of my wounds;
my neighbors stay far away.

Please read the following reference verses and fulfillment verse, then answer the questions on the following page.

REFERENCES

Psalm 31:11: *Because of all my enemies, I am the utter contempt of my neighbors and an object of dread to my closest friends—those who see me on the street flee from me.*

Job 19:13: *He has alienated my family from me; my acquaintances are completely estranged from me.*

Psalm 88:18: *You have taken from me friend and neighbor—the darkness is my closest friend.*

FULFILLMENTS

Matthew 26:56–58: *"But this has all taken place that the writings of the prophets might be fulfilled." Then all the disciples deserted him and fled. Those who had arrested Jesus took him to Caiaphas the high priest, where the teachers of the law and the elders had assembled. But Peter followed him at a distance, right up to the courtyard of the high priest. He entered and sat down with the guards to see the outcome.*

Mark 15:40–41: *Some women were watching from a distance. Among them were Mary Magdalene, Mary the mother of James the younger and of Joseph, and Salome. In Galilee these woman had followed him and cared for his needs. Many other women who had come up with him to Jerusalem were also there.*

Luke 23:49: *But all those who knew him, including the women who had followed him from Galilee, stood at a distance, watching these things.*

Psalm 38:11 Questions

I think we all may have gotten a small taste recently of how Jesus may have felt when He was abandoned by His disciples, and even the women who cared for His needs. Have you ever been shunned? Have any of your friends ever avoided you because of your faith? Did any of your friends intentionally avoid you during the COVID-19 pandemic?

Do you see any correlation between the disciples' fear of being with Jesus and any of your friends' fear of being around you during the pandemic or for any other reasons?

What reasons did people give you for not wanting to be around you?

How did that isolation make you feel?

PSALM 40:7–8

Then I said, "Here I am, I have come—it is written about me
in the scroll. I desire to do your will, my God;
your law is within my heart."

Please read the following reference verses and fulfillment verses, then answer the questions on the following page.

REFERENCES

Psalm 37:31: *The law of their God is in their hearts; their feet do not slip.*

Hebrews 10:5–10: *Therefore, when Christ came into the world, he said: "Sacrifice and offering you did not desire, but a body you prepared for me; with burnt offerings and sin offerings you were not pleased. Then I said, 'Here I am—it is written about me in the scroll—I have come to do your will, my God.'"*

Deuteronomy 17:18: *When he takes the throne of his kingdom, he is to write for himself on a scroll a copy of this law, taken from that of the Levitical priests.*

FULFILLMENTS

John 4:34: *"My food ," said Jesus, "is to do the will of him who sent me and to finish his work."*

John 17:1–8: *After Jesus said this, he looked toward heaven and prayed: "Father, the hour has come. Glorify your Son, that your Son may glorify you. For you granted him authority over all people that he might give eternal life to all those you have given him. Now this is eternal life: that they know you, the only true God, and Jesus Christ, whom you have sent. I have brought you glory on earth by finishing the work you gave me to do. And now, Father, glorify me in your presence with the glory I had with you before the world began. I have revealed you to those whom you gave me out of the world. They were yours; you gave them to me and they have obeyed your word. Now they know that everything you have given me comes from you. For I gave them the words you gave me and they accepted them. They knew with certainty that I came from you, and they believed that you sent me."*

Psalm 40:7–8 Questions

Read Psalm 37:31: *The law of their God is in their hearts; their feet do not slip.*

Do you wish to do God's will? Why? What does that look like in your life?

How do you prepare yourself to do that?

How do you know what God's will is in your life?

Has God's law penetrated your heart ?

In our fulfillment verse, John 4:34, Jesus felt "fed" by doing the will of His Father.

Do you feel fed by what you know to be Gods will? How does that show itself to you?

Do you feel comforted to know you are living in His will?

PSALM 41:9

Even my close friend, someone I trusted,
one who shared my bread, has turned against me.

Please read the reference verses and fulfillment verses, then answer the questions on the following page.

REFERENCES

2 Samuel 15:12: *While Absalom was offering sacrifices, he also sent for Ahithophel the Gilonite, David's counselor, to come from Giloh, his hometown. And so the conspiracy gained strength, and Absalom's following kept on increasing.*

Psalm 55:12–14: *If an enemy were insulting me, I could endure it; if a foe were rising against me, I could hide. But it is you, a man like myself, my companion, my close friend, with whom I once enjoyed sweet fellowship at the house of God.*

Job 19:19: *All my intimate friends detest me; those I love have turned against me.*

John 13:18: *I am not referring to all of you; I know those I have chosen. But this is to fulfill this passage of Scripture: "He who shared my bread has turned against me."*

FULFILLMENTS

Matthew 26:23–24: *Jesus replied, "The one who has dipped his hand into the bowl with me will betray me. The Son of Man will go just as it is written about him. But woe to that man who betrays the Son of Man! It would be better for him if he had not been born."*

Luke 22:48: *Jesus asked him, "Judas, are you betraying the Son of Man with a kiss?"*

Psalm 41:9 Questions

Read Psalm 55:12–14. *If an enemy were insulting me, I could endure it; if a foe were rising against me, I could hide. But it is you, a man like myself, my companion, my close friend, with whom I once enjoyed sweet fellowship at the house of God.*

Why do you think Judas sold Jesus out?

Do you think Jesus ever treated Judas differently than the other disciples?

Have you ever been betrayed by a close friend? If you had known the betrayal was coming, would you still have spent time with them? Would you have done anything differently?

PSALM 45:6–7

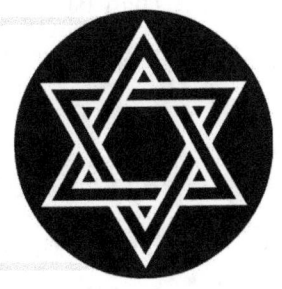

Your throne, O God, will last forever and ever; a scepter of justice will be the scepter of your kingdom. You love righteousness and hate wickedness; therefore God, your God, has set you above your companions by anointing you with the oil of joy.

(This describes the Messiah's future relationship with the Church.)

Please read these reference verses and fulfillment verses, then answer the questions on the following page.

REFERENCES

Psalm 89:27: *I will appoint him to be my firstborn, the most exalted of the kings of the earth.*

Psalm 93:2: *Your throne was established long ago; you are from all eternity.*

Isaiah 61:1: *The Spirit of the Sovereign LORD is on me, because the LORD has anointed me to proclaim good news to the poor.**

FULFILLMENT

Hebrews 1:8–9: *But about the Son he says, "Your throne, O God, will last for ever and ever; a scepter of justice will be the scepter of your kingdom. You have loved righteousness and hated wickedness; therefore God, your God, has set you above your companions by anointing you with the oil of joy."*

---

* Fulfillment of this Scripture: Luke 4:16–21 says, *He went to Nazareth, where he had been brought up, and on the Sabbath day he went into the synagogue, as was his custom. He stood up to read, and the scroll of the prophet Isaiah was handed to him. Unrolling it, he found the place where it is written: "The Spirit of The Lord is on me, because he has anointed me to proclaim good news to the poor. He has sent me to proclaim freedom for the prisoners and recovery of sight for the blind, to set the oppressed free, to proclaim the year of the Lord's favor." Then he rolled up the scroll, gave it back to the attendant and sat down. The eyes of everyone in the synagogue were fastened on him. He began by saying to them, "Today this scripture is fulfilled in your hearing."*

Psalm 45:6–7 Questions

Please read Luke 4:22–30: *All spoke well of him and were amazed at the gracious words that came from his lips. "Isn't this Joseph's son?" they asked. Jesus said to them, "Surely you will quote this proverb to me: 'Physician, heal yourself!' And you will tell me, 'Do here in your hometown what we have heard that you did in Capernaum.'"*

"Truly I tell you," he continued, "no prophet is accepted in his hometown. I assure you that there were many widows in Israel in Elijah's time, when the sky was shut for three and a half years and there was a severe famine throughout the land. Yet Elijah was not sent to any of them, but to a widow in Zarephath in the region of Sidon. And there were many in Israel with leprosy in the time of Elisha the prophet, yet not one of them was cleansed, but only Naaman the Syrian." All the people in the synagogue were furious when they heard this. They got up, drove him out of the town, and took him to the brow of the hill on which the town was built, in order to throw him off the cliff. But he walked right through the crowd and went on his way.

By their reaction, do you think the others in the synagogue *really* heard what Jesus said?

How could they speak so well of Jesus at first and then become so angry?

They tried to throw Jesus off the cliff. What do you think angered them so?

LESSON 4

PSALM 55:12–14

If an enemy were insulting me, I could endure it; if a foe were rising against me, I could hide. But it is you, a man like myself, my companion, my close friend, with whom I once enjoyed sweet fellowship at the house of God.

Please read the following references and fulfilment scriptures, then answer the questions on the following page.

REFERENCES

Psalm 41:9: *Even my close friend, someone I trusted, one who shared my bread, has turned against me.*

Job 19:19: *All my intimate friends detest me; those I love have turned against me.*

FULFILLMENTS

Matthew 26:14–16: *Then one of the Twelve—the one called Judas Iscariot—went to the chief priests and asked, "What are you willing to give me if I deliver him over to you?" So they counted out for him thirty pieces of silver. From then on Judas watched for an opportunity to hand him over.*

Matthew 26:23–24: *Jesus replied, "The one who has dipped his hand into the bowl with me will betray me. The Son of Man will go just as it is written about him. But woe to the man who betrays the Son of Man! It would be better for him if he had not been born."*

Matthew 26:47–50: *While he was still speaking, Judas, one of the Twelve, arrived. With him was a large crowd armed with swords and clubs, sent from the chief priests and the elders of the people. Now the betrayer had arranged a signal with them: "The one I kiss is the man; arrest him." Going at once to Jesus, Judas said, "Greetings, Rabbi!" and kissed him.*

Luke 22:20–23: *In the same way, after the supper he took the cup, saying, "This cup is the new covenant in my blood, which is poured out for you. But the hand of him who is going to betray me is with mine on the table. The Son of Man will go as it has been decreed. But woe to that man who betrays him." They began to question among themselves which of them it might be who would do this.*

Luke 22:48: *But Jesus asked him, "Judas, are you betraying the Son of Man with a kiss?"*

John 13:18: *I am not referring to all of you; I know those I have chosen. But this is to fulfill this passage of Scripture: "He who shared my bread has turned against me."*

John 18:2–5: *Now Judas, who betrayed him, knew the place, because Jesus had often met there with his disciples. So Judas came to the garden, guiding a detachment of soldiers and some officials from the chief priests and the Pharisees. They were carrying torches, lanterns and weapons. Jesus, knowing all that was going to happen to him, went out and asked them, "Who is it you want?" "Jesus of Nazareth," they replied. "I am he," Jesus said. (And Judas the traitor was standing there with them.)*

Psalm 55:12–14 Questions

These are the same references and fulfillments as Psalm 41:9. It referred to Jesus being betrayed by Judas, a close friend. This Psalm refers to David being betrayed by his own son, Absalom. Could David's pain have been even worse because he didn't know it was going to happen? Jesus did know exactly what was coming.

In 2 Samuel 18:33, David wept and exclaimed, *"If only I had died instead of you."* Before Absalom was killed, do you think David's pain at the betrayal could compare to losing a child to the culture, to addiction, or to being self-centered? If so, how?

Is it worse to be betrayed by your own family member or a close friend?

Have you ever been betrayed by a friend or a family member? If yes, can you share with us about it?

How did you move on from the pain?

PSALM 68:18

When you ascended on high, you took many captives;
you received gifts from people, even from the rebellious—
that you, LORD God, might dwell there.

Please read the following reference and the fulfillment verses for Psalm 68:18, then answer the questions on the following page.

REFERENCE

Judges 5:12: *Wake up, wake up, Deborah! Wake up, wake up, break out in song! Arise, Barak!* * *Take captive your captives, O son of Abinoam.*

FULFILLMENTS

Ephesians 4:7–10: *But to each one of us grace has been given as Christ apportioned it. This is why it says, "When he ascended on high, he took many captives and gave gifts to his people." (What does "he ascended" mean except that he also descended into the lower, earthly regions? He who descended is the very one who ascended higher than all the heavens, in order to fill the whole universe.)*

---

* *Barak* means "blessed" or "to kneel."

Luke 24:50–51: *When he had led them out to the vicinity of Bethany, he lifted up his hands and blessed them. While he was blessing them, he left them and was taken up into heaven.*

Acts 1:9–11: *After he said this, he was taken up before their very eyes, and a cloud hid him from their sight. They were looking intently up into the sky as he was going, when suddenly two men dressed in white stood beside them. "Men of Galilee," they said, "why do you stand there looking into the sky? This same Jesus, who has been taken from you into heaven, will come back in the same way you have seen him go into heaven."*

Psalm 68:18 Questions

Please read Judges 5:12.

Many great conquerors in history led their captives in victory as well. *"He led captives in his train by breaking the power of sin and Satan."* There were two compartments in hell before the death of Christ. One for unbelievers, where they were to suffer. The other was a place of comfort by Abraham for people who believed in the fulfillment of Gods promise. We know that Christ is Lord of all: past, present, future, heaven, Hades, hell.

Please read Acts1:1–11. *"You received gifts from men"*

Jesus also left gifts for men.

Explain *Pentecost* in your own words.

When the apostles received their power, Jesus gave them a specific command. What was that command?

How long was Jesus on earth after his resurrection and before his ascension?

Can you find some Scripture references about Jesus' second coming being like his ascension?

PSALM 69:8

I am a foreigner to my own family,
a stranger to my own mother's children.

Please read the reference verse, then the fulfillment verse, and answer the questions on the following page.

REFERENCE

Isaiah 53:3: *He was despised and rejected by mankind, a man of suffering, and familiar with pain. Like one from whom people hide their faces he was despised, and we held him in low esteem.*

FULFILLMENT

John 7:3–5: *Jesus' brothers said to him, "Leave Galilee and go to Judea, so that your disciples there may see the works you do. No one who wants to become a public figure acts in secret. Since you are doing these things, show yourself to the world." For even his own brothers did not believe in him.*

Psalm 69:8 Questions

Read Isaiah 53:3: *He was despised and rejected by mankind, a man of suffering, and familiar with pain. Like one from whom people hide their faces he was despised, and we held him in low esteem.*

James, Jesus' brother, eventually became a leader in the church, but his family did not believe in him for many years. Jesus knew this would happen, but how would you have felt? Would you have been disheartened if you came from a small town and no one there believed you could accomplish anything?

Without your family's support or belief in you, could you be strong enough in your faith to continue in God's work?

Could you continue to be obedient to God if everyone close to you scoffed at you and the things you were doing?

How do you stay strong in your faith amidst the doubters, the conflict, and this current culture?

PSALM 69:9

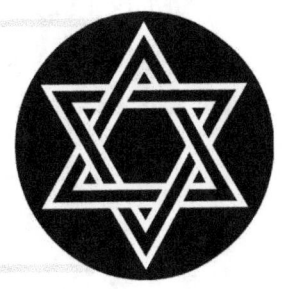

Zeal for your house consumes me,
and the insults of those who insult you fall on me.

Please read the reference verses and fulfillment verses below, then answer the questions on the following page.

REFERENCES

Matthew 21:12–13: *Jesus entered the temple courts and drove out all who were buying and selling there. He overturned the tables of the money changers and the benches of those selling doves. "It is written," he said to them, "'My house will be called a house of prayer,' but you are making it a 'den of robbers.'"*

Psalm 89:50–51: *Remember, Lord, how your servant has been mocked, how I bear in my heart the taunts of all the nations, the taunts with which your enemies, LORD, have mocked, with which they have mocked every step of your anointed one.*

FULFILLMENTS

John 2:16–17: *To those who sold doves he said, "Get these out of here! Stop turning my Father's house into a market!" His disciples remembered that it is written: "Zeal for your house will consume me."*

Mark 15:29–30: *Those who passed by hurled insults at him, shaking their heads and saying, "So! You who are going to destroy the temple and build it in three days, come down from the cross and save yourself."*

Psalm 69:9 Questions

Jesus took evil acts in the temple as an insult to God. They were interfering with worship. How many times and when did Jesus confront the money changers in the temple?

Read John 2:13–17.

Read Matthew 21:12–13.

Is anything in your church hindering worship? If so, describe what is getting in the way.

Can your church truly be called a house of prayer?

Is your church compromising the Word of God to attract more people?

Please read this fulfillment scripture again: Mark 15:29–30. Did Jesus say, "I will destroy this man-made temple and in three days will build another, not made by man?"

What did Jesus mean in those words that the Jews misunderstood?

Psalm 69:21

They put gall in my food and gave me vinegar for my thirst.

Please read the reference verses and the fulfillment verse, then answer the questions on the following page.

REFERENCES

Matthew 27:34: *There they offered Jesus wine to drink, mixed with gall; but after tasting it, he refused to drink it.*

Mark 15:23: *Then they offered him wine mixed with myrrh, but he did not take it.*

FULFILLMENT

John 19:28–30: *Later, knowing that everything had now been finished, and so that Scripture would be fulfilled, Jesus said, "I am thirsty ." A jar of wine vinegar was there, so they soaked a sponge in it, put the sponge on a stalk of the hyssop plant, and lifted it to Jesus' lips. When he had received the drink, Jesus said, "It is finished." With that, he bowed his head and gave up his spirit.*

Psalm 69:21 Questions

This Scripture* directly points to the fact that Jesus could not say, "It is finished" until this Scripture was fulfilled. Again, be aware that David wrote this psalm at least one thousand years before Jesus was even born.

What is gall?

What is vinegar, and why is it significant to Jesus' death?

Why did the soldiers put gall or myrrh in the sponge? To make it bitter. The Roman custom was to give it to the dying to render them insensible to pain; basically, it acted as an anesthetic. Do you think that's why they gave it to Jesus?

---

* Matthew Henry commentary on Psalm 69 says, "See how particularly the sufferings of Christ were foretold, which proves the Scripture to be the Word of God, and how exactly the predictions were fulfilled in Jesus Christ, which proves him to be the true Messiah. This is he that should come, and we are to look for no other."

Could it have been to help Him, or was it meant to make Him more miserable?

Why do you think Jesus refused to drink it after He said, "I thirst"?

LESSON 5

PSALM 72:1-4

*Endow the king with your justice, O God, the royal son
with your righteousness. May he judge your people in
righteousness, your afflicted ones with justice. May the
mountains bring prosperity to the people, the hills the fruit
of righteousness. May he defend the afflicted among
the people and save the children of the needy;
may he crush the oppressor.*

Please read the reference and fulfillment verses below, then answer the questions on the following page.

REFERENCES

Romans 3:21–22: *But now apart from the law the righteousness of God has been made known, to which the Law and Prophets testify. This righteousness is given through faith in Jesus Christ to all who believe.*

Matthew 19:14: *Jesus said, "Let the little children come to me, and do not hinder them, for the kingdom of heaven belongs to such as these."*

2 Timothy 4:8: *Now there is in store for me the crown of righteousness, which the Lord, the righteous Judge, will award to me on that day—and not only to me, but also to all who have longed for his appearing.*

FULFILLMENTS

Romans 1:17: *For in the gospel the righteousness of God is revealed—a righteousness that is by faith from first to last, just as it is written: "The righteous will live by faith."*

Acts 17:31: *For he has set a day when he will judge the world with justice by the man he has appointed. He has given proof of this to all men by raising him from the dead.*

Psalm 72:1–4 Questions

These four verses in Psalm 72 describe the perfect leader. Are all of the leaders in your life righteous and just? Or could they use your prayer and encouragement to be better leaders? Ask God to show them that good leaders need Him in their lives.

Read Romans 3:21–22. In your own words, explain what this means to you, and what it means to us as Christians.

Read Matthew 19:14. Cite some Scripture references where Jesus refers to little children and how we should be like them.

In our fulfillment verse, Romans 1:17, what does Paul mean by the righteous will live by faith?

Psalm 72:8–11

May he rule from sea to sea and from the River to the ends of the earth. May the desert tribes bow before him and his enemies lick the dust. May the kings of Tarshish and of distant shores bring tribute to him. May the kings of Sheba and Seba present him gifts. May all kings bow down to him and all nations serve him.

Please read the reference verse and fulfillment verses below, then answer the questions on the following page.

REFERENCE

Matthew 25:32–33: *All the nations will be gathered before him, and he will separate the people one from another as a shepherd separates the sheep from the goats. He will put the sheep on his right and the goats on his left.*

FULFILLMENTS

Matthew 2:9–12: *After they had heard the king, they went on their way, and the star they had seen when it rose went ahead of them until it stopped over the place where the child was. When they saw the star, they were overjoyed. On coming to the house, they saw the child with his mother Mary, and they bowed down and worshipped him. Then they opened their treasures and presented him with gifts of gold, frankincense and myrrh. And having been warned in a dream not to go back to Herod, they returned to their country by another route.*

Philippians 2:9–11: *Therefore God exalted him to the highest place and gave him the name that is above every name, that at the name of Jesus every knee should bow, in heaven and on earth and under the earth, and every tongue acknowledge that Jesus Christ is Lord, to the glory of God the Father.*

Revelation 15:4: *Who will not fear you, Lord, and bring glory to your name? For you alone are holy. All nations will come and worship before you, for your righteous acts have been revealed.*

Psalm 72:8–11 Questions

Read Ezekiel 34:11–16. What does God say about tending His flock? How will He do it?

Read Matthew 25:32–33. How do you think Jesus means to separate the righteous from the unrighteous? The believers from the unbelievers? Why were the sheep separated from goats? They very often grazed together.

Read the first fulfillment verses, Matthew 2:9–11. Even Jesus' humble birth was preparing Him for His life as a humble servant. Kings from distant lands were bowing to Him and bringing Him gifts. Then God gave Joseph a dream and told him Herod was looking for them to kill the child, and they must flee. A very humble beginning indeed.

Read the second fulfillment verses, Philippians 2:9–11. Personally it gives me great comfort to know that "every knee will bow," but it also gives me great stress for all of the people who will not turn to Jesus. Do you pray daily for the unbelievers in your life and for those you don't know? Has God ever sent you to speak to anyone about Him? Did you obey? If yes, what were the results ?

In Revelation 15:4, the third fulfillment verse talks about all nations. In our world today, do you see nations coming together for good? Does it even seem possible that any would?

PSALM 72:12-14

For he will deliver the needy who cry out, the afflicted who have no one to help. He will take pity on the weak and the needy and save the needy from death. He will rescue them from oppression and violence, for precious is their blood in his sight.

Please read the reference verses and the fulfillment verse below, then answer the questions on the following page.

REFERENCES

Luke 4:18–19: *The Spirit of The Lord is on me, because he has anointed me to proclaim the good news to the poor. He has sent me to proclaim freedom for the prisoners and recovery of sight for the blind, to set the oppressed free, to proclaim the year of the Lord's favor.*

Luke 18:38–42: *He called out, "Jesus, Son of David, have mercy on me!" Those who led the way rebuked him and told him to be quiet, but he shouted all the more, "Son of David, have mercy on me!" Jesus stopped and ordered the man to be brought to him. When he came near, Jesus asked him, "What do you want me to do for you?" "Lord, I want to see," he replied. Jesus said to him, "Receive your sight; your faith has healed you."*

Matthew 17:14–18: *When they came to the crowd, a man approached Jesus and knelt before him. "Lord, have mercy on my son," he said. "He has seizures and is suffering greatly. He often falls into the fire or into the water. I brought him to your disciples, but they could not heal him." "You unbelieving and perverse generation," Jesus replied, "how long shall I stay with you? How long shall I put up with you? Bring the boy here to me." Jesus rebuked the demon, and it came out of the boy, and he was healed from that moment.*

Mark 5:1–9: *They went across the lake to the region of the Gerasenes. When Jesus got out of the boat, a man with an impure spirit came from the tombs to meet him. This man lived in the tombs, and no one could bind him anymore, not even with a chain. For he had often been chained hand and foot, but he tore the chains apart and broke the irons on his feet. No one was strong enough to subdue him. Night and day among the tombs and in the hills he would cry out and cut himself with stones. When he saw Jesus from a distance, he ran and fell on his knees in front of him. He shouted at the top of his voice, "What do you want with me, Jesus, Son of the Most High God? In God's name don't torture me!" For Jesus had said to him, "Come out of this man, you impure spirit!" Then Jesus asked him, "What is your name?" "My name is Legion," he replied, "for we are many."*

FULFILLMENT

Luke 7:21–22: *At that very time Jesus cured many who had diseases, sicknesses and evil spirits, and gave sight to many who were blind. So he replied to the messengers, "Go back and report to John what you have seen and heard: The blind receive sight, the lame walk, those who have leprosy are cleansed, the deaf hear, the dead are raised, and the good news is proclaimed to the poor.*

Psalm 72:12–14 Questions

The needy, the afflicted, the weak, and the oppressed are all precious to God. What does this portion of Psalm 72 teach us about the Messiah?

What does it teach us about how we should behave?

Read Luke 4:18–19, Luke 18:38–42, Matthew 14:18, and Mark 5:1–9.

All of these acts of Jesus were real, physical proofs of him being the Messiah. His contemporaries witnessed these and many more deeds and carefully recorded them for us.

Jesus repeatedly taught—in these examples and many more—that we are to step up in His place and reach out to the poor and needy. Do you do enough for those who are in need? Does your church do enough? Is your church discerning of who needs help? Is there a protocol in place to help your church avoid enabling some of the needy who might be taking advantage of the church's good will?

Read the fulfillment verses again: Luke 7:21–22.

What is the context? Who were the messengers? Who sent them?

PSALM 72:17

May his name endure forever; may it continue as long as the sun.
All nations will be blessed through him,
and they will call him blessed.

Please read the reference and fulfillment verses, then answer the questions on the following page.

REFERENCES

Psalm 89:35–37: *Once for all, I have sworn by my holiness—and I will not lie to David—that his line will continue forever and his throne endure before me like the sun; it will be established forever like the moon, the faithful witness in the sky.*

Genesis 12:3: *I will bless those who bless you, and whoever curses you I will curse; and all the peoples on earth will be blessed through you.*

Matthew 12:21: *In his name the nations will put their hope.*

FULFILLMENTS

Philippians 2:9–11: *Therefore God exalted him to the highest place and gave him the name that is above every name, that at the name of Jesus every knee should bow, in heaven and on earth and under the earth, and every tongue acknowledge that Jesus Christ is Lord, to the glory of God the Father.*

Acts 3:25: *And you are heirs of the prophets and of the covenant God made with your fathers. He said to Abraham, "Through your offspring all peoples on earth will be blessed."*

Galatians 3:8–9: *Scripture foresaw that God would justify the Gentiles by faith, and announced the gospel in advance to Abraham: "All nations will be blessed through you." So those who rely on faith are blessed along with Abraham, the man of faith.*

Psalm 72:17 Questions

Read Revelation 21:23. The city does not need the sun or the moon to shine on it, for the glory of God gives it light, and the Lamb is its lamp.

Read Psalm 89:35–37.

What do these Scriptures tell you about the *sun*?

What do these Scriptures tell you about the *Son*?

Throughout history, we have seen ungodly nations thrive and then fall. Do you notice God's intervention? Do you think the ungodly notice it?

Do you believe that God always keeps His promises? Can you cite some Biblical examples? Can you cite some examples from your own life?

PSALM 78:2

*I will open my mouth with a parable; I
will utter hidden things, things from of old.*

Please read all of the reference and fulfillment verses, then answer the
questions on the following page.

REFERENCES

Deuteronomy 29:29: *The secret things belong to the Lord our God, but the things
revealed belong to us and to our children forever, that we may follow all the words
of this law.*

Romans 16:25–27: *Now to him who is able to establish you in accordance with my
gospel, the message I proclaim about Jesus Christ, in keeping with the revelation of
the mystery hidden for long ages past, but now revealed and made known through
the prophetic writings by the command of the eternal God, so that all the Gentiles
might come to the obedience that comes from faith—to the only wise God be glory
forever through Jesus Christ! Amen.*

1 Corinthians 2:7: *No, we declare God's wisdom, a mystery that has been hidden
and that God destined for our glory before time began.*

Ephesians 3:9: *And to make plain to everyone the administration of this mystery, which for ages past was kept hidden in God, who created all things.*

Colossians 1:26–27: *The mystery that has been kept hidden for ages and generations, but is now disclosed to the Lord's people. To them God has chosen to make known among the Gentiles the glorious riches of this mystery, which is Christ in you, the hope of glory.*

FULFILLMENTS

Matthew 13:10–13: *The disciples came to him and asked, "Why do you speak to the people in parables?" He replied, "Because the knowledge of the secrets of the kingdom of heaven has been given to you, but not to them. Whoever has will be given more, and they will have an abundance. Whoever does not have, even what they have will be taken away from them. This is why I speak to them in parables: 'Though seeing, they do not see; though hearing, they do not hear or understand.'"*

Matthew 13:34–35: *Jesus spoke all these things to the crowd in parables; he did not say anything to them without using a parable. So was fulfilled what was spoken through the prophet: "I will open my mouth in parables, I will utter things hidden since the creation of the world."*

Psalm 78:2 Questions

Asaph wrote Psalm 50 and Psalms 73–83. He was a composer and considered a "seer." Clearly, this verse is a prophecy of the Messiah. (Also see Psalm 80:14–15, 17.)

Read Deuteronomy 29:29. The secret things belong to the Lord our God, but the things revealed belong to us and to our children forever so that we may follow all the words of this law.

Read 1 Corinthians 2:7: *No, we declare God's wisdom, a mystery that has been hidden and that God destined for our glory before time began.*

Read Ephesians 3:9: *And to make plain to everyone the administration of this mystery, which for ages past was kept hidden in God, who created all things.*

We can only thank God for revealing the things to us that He has through His Holy Word, acknowledging that there are things we will never understand. Have you ever read a Bible verse at least fifty times, then all of a sudden it was like a light bulb went off? You finally got it because God knew the time was right to reveal that bit of knowledge to you. Perhaps that bit of knowledge, that new revelation, was for you to share with someone else. Can you share a time here when that happened to you? Or perhaps a friend had a revelation or message for you?

Read our fulfillment verses, Matthew 13:10–13 and Matthew 13:34–35.

How does Jesus explain speaking in parables? Do you think He was trying to hide knowledge from people?

Before I was a believer, I didn't understand a single Psalm or Proverb that I read. Immediately upon receiving the Holy Spirit, the Lord gave me a voracious appetite for His Holy Word. Now it makes sense to me, and I understand it.

Is there a parable that you don't quite understand? Do you care to share it? Maybe someone in the group can help you understand it.

LESSON 6

PSALM 80:14–15

Return to us, God Almighty! Look down from heaven and see!
Watch over this vine, the root your right hand has planted,
the son you have raised up for yourself.

Please read the reference verses and the fulfillment verse, then answer the questions on the following page.

REFERENCES

Isaiah 63:15: *Look down from heaven and see, from your lofty throne, holy and glorious.*

Isaiah 5:7: *The vineyard of the LORD Almighty is the nation of Israel, and the people of Judah are the vines he delighted in.*

FULFILLMENT

John 15:1–8: *I am the true vine, and my Father is the gardener. He cuts off every branch in me that bears no fruit, while every branch that does bear fruit he prunes so that it will be even more fruitful. You are already clean because of the word I have spoken to you. Remain in me, as I also remain in you. No branch can bear fruit by itself; it must remain in the vine. Neither can you bear fruit unless you remain in me. I am the vine; you are the branches. If you remain in me and I in you, you will bear much fruit; apart from me you can do nothing. If you do not remain in me, you are like a branch that is thrown away and withers; such branches are picked up, thrown into the fire and burned. If you remain in me and my words remain in you, ask whatever you wish, and it will be done for you. This is to my Father's glory, that you bear much fruit, showing yourselves to be my disciples.*

Psalm 80:14–15 Questions

Read Isaiah 5:7. The vineyard of the Lord Almighty is the house of Israel, and the men of Judah are the garden of his delight.

In your own words, what does this Scripture say to you?

Are you actively bearing fruit for the kingdom of God? If so, how?

Do you know the joy of sharing God's Word with an unbeliever?

Are you happy when you can plant even a small seed?

Do you pray for God to give you a burden for the lost?

Would you like more information about sharing your faith?*

---

* I recommend reading *Share Jesus Without Fear* by William Fay and Ralph Hodge and *Secret to an Open Door* by David A. Morel.

PSALM 80:17

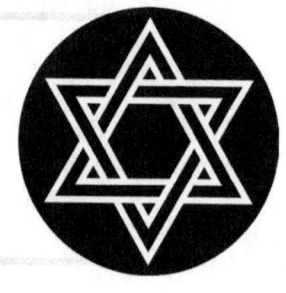

Let your right hand rest on the man at your right hand,
the son of man you have raised up for yourself.

Please read the reference verses and fulfillment verse below, then answer the questions on the following page.

REFERENCES

Psalm 110:1: *The LORD says to my Lord: "Sit at my right hand until I make your enemies a footstool for your feet."*

1 Corinthians 15:25–28: *For he must reign until he has put all his enemies under his feet. The last enemy to be destroyed is death. For he "has put everything under his feet." Now when it says that "everything" has been put under him, it is clear that this does not include God himself, who put everything under Christ. When he has done this, then the Son himself will be made subject to him who put everything under him, so that God may be all in all.*

FULFILLMENT

Hebrews 10:11–14: *Day after day every priest stands and performs his religious duties; again and again he offers the same sacrifices, which can never take away sins. But when this priest had offered for all time one sacrifice for sins, he sat down at the right hand of God, and since that time he waits for his enemies to be made his footstool. For by one sacrifice he has made perfect forever those who are being made holy.*

Key takeaway: These are the Messiah's credentials, so he must be equal to God.

Psalm 80:17 Questions

Read 1 Corinthians 15:25–28. World events may seem out of control, but what does this Scripture tell you about who is really in control of all things. Can you and do you rely on that?

Read Hebrews 10, focusing on verses 11–14, our fulfillment verses, and write what comes to mind about the Messiah.

Read Matthew 26:64: *But I say to all of you: From now on you will see the Son of Man sitting at the right hand of the Mighty One and coming on the clouds of heaven.*

Do you find comfort in knowing Jesus will return, and that we will not need to question who He is? Can you cite some other Scripture references that really speak to you about the second coming?

From BSF Revelation study:

There were no chairs in the tabernacle because the work of the ancient priests was never done. They could never sit down and know their work was completed.

"Day after day every priest stands and performs his religious duties; again and again he offers the same sacrifices, which can never take away sins. But when this priest had offered for all time one sacrifice for sins, he sat down at the right hand of God, and since that time he waits for his enemies to be made his footstool. For by one sacrifice he has made perfect forever those who are being made holy."

What high priest was able to sit at the right hand of God? Why was he qualified?

When did He take away the sins of the world? Did he even take away your sins?

Psalm 89:3–4

*You said, "I have made a covenant with my chosen one, I have
sworn to David my servant, I will establish your line forever and
make your throne firm through all generations."*

Please read the following references and fulfillment scriptures, then answer
the questions pertaining to this Psalm.

REFERENCES

1 Kings 8:16: *Since the day I brought my people Israel out of Egypt, I have not
chosen a city in any tribe of Israel to have a temple built so that my Name might be
there, but I have chosen David to rule my people Israel.*

Isaiah 9:6–7: *For to us a child is born, to us a son is given, and the government
will be on his shoulders. And he will be called Wonderful Counselor, Mighty God,
Everlasting Father, Prince of Peace. Of the greatness of his government and peace
there will be no end. He will reign on David's throne and over his kingdom,
establishing and upholding it with justice and righteousness from that time on and
forever. The zeal of the LORD Almighty will accomplish this.*

FULFILLMENTS

Matthew 1:17: *Thus there were fourteen generations in all from Abraham to David, fourteen from David to the exile to Babylon, and fourteen from the exile to the Christ..*

Luke 1:30–33: *But the angel said to her, "Do not be afraid, Mary; you have found favor with God. You will conceive and give birth to a son, and you are to call him Jesus. He will be great and will be called the Son of the Most High. The Lord God will give him the throne of his father David, and he will reign over Jacob's descendants forever; his kingdom will never end."**

From the following Scripture, explain the curse on Jechoniah and explain in your own words why Jesus could not have been descended from Joseph.

The curse on Jechoniah is found in Jeremiah 22:24–30, also known as Jehoiachin. In 2 Kings 24:8–9 it says, *Jehoiachin was eighteen years old when he became king, and he reigned in Jerusalem three months. His mother's name was Nehushta daughter of Elnathan; she was from Jerusalem. He did evil in the eyes of the LORD, just as his father had done.*

Jeremiah 22:21: *I warned you when you felt secure, but you said, "I will not listen!" This has been your way from your youth; you have not obeyed me.*

Jeremiah 22:24–30: *"As surely as I live," declares the LORD, "even if you, Jehoiachin son of Jehoiakim king of Judah, were a signet ring on my right hand, I would still pull you off. I will deliver you into the hands of those who want to kill you, those you fear—Nebuchadnezzar king of Babylon and the Babylonians. I will hurl you and the mother who gave you birth into another country, where neither of you was*

---

* Jesus was not descended from Solomon (through Jeconiah) but through Nathan to Mary, thus avoiding the curse on Jeconiah. Jesus was of the house of David through Mary.

born, and there you both will die. You will never come back to the land you long to return to."

> *Is this man Jehoiachin a despised, broken pot,*
> > *an object no one wants?*
> *Why will he and his children be hurled out,*
> > *cast into a land they do not know?*
> *Oh land, land, land,*
> > *hear the word of the LORD!*
> *This is what the LORD says:*
> *"Record this man as if childless,*
> > *a man who will not prosper in his lifetime,*
> *for none of his offspring will prosper,*
> > *none will sit on the throne of David*
> > *or rule anymore in Judah."*

Psalm 89:3–4 continued

Jesus' genealogy:

Read Matthew 1:1-16. These passages show the complete geneology of Jesus, from Abraham through Mary.

Matthew mentions this to show that Jesus was *not* Joseph's son

Read Luke 3:23-37. In these passages Luke shows Jesus's geneology from Adam.

Joseph was the only one mentioned, but in the Greek translation Joseph was the only one mentioned in the entire genealogy without the definite article "the" in front of his name. This could only mean that this was not really Joseph's genealogy but Mary's. It was the husband's name that was used, according to Jewish law. Without "the" in front of his name, it meant "not of him but of his wife Mary." The Talmud mentions Miriam daughter of Heli.

Matthew showed why Jesus *could not* be king if he really was Joseph's son. Luke shows why Jesus *could* be king because he was descended from David through Mary.

Psalm 89:3–4 Questions

Psalm 89 speaks principally to the Davidic covenant. The Davidic covenant shows God's faithfulness in promising David his line will continue forever.

Why do you think Matthew began his gospel with the genealogy of Jesus?

Could Jesus have been king if he was Joseph's son?

In your own words, explain the curse on Jehoiachin and why Jesus could not have been descended from Joseph.

Psalm 89:35-37

Once for all, I have sworn by my holiness—and I will not lie to David—that his line will continue forever and his throne endure before me like the sun; it will be established like the moon, the faithful witness in the sky.

Please read the reference and fulfillment verses below, then answer the questions on the following page.

REFERENCE

2 Samuel 7:12–13: *When your days are over and you rest with your ancestors, I will raise up your offspring to succeed you, your own flesh and blood, and I will establish his kingdom. He is the one who will build a house for my Name, and I will establish the throne of his kingdom forever.*

FULFILLMENTS

Luke 1:31–33: *You will conceive and give birth to a son, and you are to call him Jesus. He will be great and will be called the Son of the Most High. The Lord God will give him the throne of his father David, and he will reign over Jacob's descendants forever; his kingdom will never end.*

Revelation 22:3–5: *No longer will there be any curse. The throne of God and the Lamb will be in the city, and his servants will serve him. They will see his face, and his name will be on their foreheads. There will be no more night. They will not need the light of a lamp or the light of the sun, for the Lord God will give them light. And they will reign for ever and ever.*

Psalm 89:35–37 Questions

Read 2 Samuel 7:12–17. To whom was this revelation given?

What did you learn about God in these verses?

Read 2 Samuel 7:18–27.

How did David respond?

Was David more concerned about God's reputation or his own?

Our fulfillment verses are Luke 1:31–33.

This prophecy could only have been fulfilled by Jesus. The entire line of succession from David pointed straight to Jesus. His kingdom will never end.

Read our second fulfillment verses Revelation 22:3–5: *No longer will there be any curse. The throne of God and the Lamb will be in the city, and his servants will serve him. They will see his face, and his name will be on their foreheads. There will be no more night. They will not need the light of a lamp or the light of the sun, for the Lord God will give them light. And they will reign for ever and ever.*

Do these verses give you hope? Can you explain why?

Key takeaway: And they will reign for ever and ever!

Psalm 89:50–51

Remember, Lord, how your servant has been mocked, how I bear in my heart the taunts of all the nations, the taunts with which your enemies, LORD, have mocked, with which they have mocked every step of your anointed one.

Please read the reference verse and fulfillment verses, then answer the questions on the following page.

REFERENCE

Mark 10:33–34: *"We are going up to Jerusalem," he said, "and the Son of Man will be delivered over to the chief priests and teachers of the law. They will condemn him to death and hand him over to the Gentiles, who will mock him and spit on him, flog him and kill him. Three days later he will rise."*

FULFILLMENTS

Matthew 27:28–31: *They stripped him and put a scarlet robe on him, and then twisted together a crown of thorns and set it on his head. They put a staff in his right hand. Then they knelt in front of him and mocked him. "Hail, King of the Jews!" they said. They spit on him, and took the staff and struck him on the head again and again. After they had mocked him, they took off the robe and put his own clothes on him.*

Luke 22:63–65: *The men who were guarding Jesus began mocking and beating him. They blindfolded him and demanded, "Prophesy! Who hit you?" And they said many other insulting things to him.*

Luke 23:11: *Then Herod and his soldiers ridiculed and mocked him. Dressing him in an elegant robe, they sent him back to Pilate.*

John 1:45–46: *Philip found Nathanael and told him, "We have found the one Moses wrote about in the Law, and about whom the prophets also wrote—Jesus of Nazareth, the son of Joseph." "Nazareth! Can anything good come from there?" Nathanael asked.*

Psalm 89:50–51 Questions

Read Mark 10:32–45.

How many times had Jesus explained His forthcoming death and resurrection to the disciples?

Why do you think they didn't get it?

How did they react to hearing it again in these verses?

Read John 1:45–46. Jesus was also being mocked very often just for being from Nazareth. What cities today do you think could compare to Nazareth? Maybe Harlem, Detroit, or Memphis?

LESSON 7

PSALM 91:11–12

*For he will command his angels concerning you to guard you in
all your ways; they will lift you up in their hands, so that you will
not strike your foot against a stone.*

Please read all of the reference verses and fulfillment verses below, then answer the questions on the following page.

REFERENCES

Psalm 34:7: *The angel of the LORD encamps around those who fear him, and he delivers them.*

Matthew 2:13: *When they had gone, an angel of the Lord appeared to Joseph in a dream. "Get up," he said," take the child and his mother and escape to Egypt. Stay there until I tell you, for Herod is going to search for the child to kill him."*

Matthew 2:19–20: *After Herod died, an angel of the Lord appeared in a dream to Joseph in Egypt and said, "Get up, take the child and his mother and go to the land of Israel, for those who were trying to take the child's life are dead."*

Matthew 4:10–11: *Jesus said to him, "Away from me, Satan! For it is written: 'Worship the Lord your God, and serve him only.'" Then the devil left him, and angels came and attended him.*

Luke 22:42–43: *"Father, if you are willing, take this cup from me; yet not my will, but yours be done." An angel from heaven appeared to him and strengthened him.*

FULFILLMENTS

Matthew 28:2: *There was a violent earthquake, for an angel of the Lord came down from heaven and, going to the tomb, rolled back the stone and sat on it.*

Matthew 4:6: *"If you are the son of God," he said, "throw yourself down. For it is written: "He will command his angels concerning you, and they will lift you up in their hands, so that you will not strike your foot against a stone.""*

Psalm 91:11–12 Questions

Read all reference verses.

Jesus was protected by angels from the moment of His divine conception to His resurrection. Find other references to this fact and list them here.

Read Psalm 34:7. Has there been a time in your life (or many times) that you know angels were encamped around you?

Did you pray for protection, or did God provide it before you knew you needed it?

Has anyone ever used Scripture against you? How did you respond?

PSALM 96:12–13

Let the fields be jubilant, and everything in them; let all the trees of the forest sing for joy. Let all creation rejoice before the Lord, for he comes, he comes to judge the earth. He will judge the world in righteousness and the peoples in his faithfulness.

Please read the reference verses and the fulfillment verse, then answer the questions on the following page.

REFERENCES

1 Thessalonians 1:10: *To wait for his Son from heaven, whom he raised from the dead—Jesus, who rescues us from the coming wrath.*

John 5:27–30: *And he has given him authority to judge because he is the Son of Man. "Do not be amazed at this, for a time is coming when all who are in their graves will hear his voice and come out—those who have done what is good will rise to live, and those who have done evil will rise to be condemned. By myself I can do nothing; I judge only as I hear, and my judgement is just, for I seek not to please myself but him who sent me."*

Acts 17:31: *For he has set a day when he will judge the world with justice by the man he has appointed. He has given proof of this to everyone by raising him from the dead.*

FULFILLMENT

Revelation 19:11–15: *I saw heaven standing open and there before me was a white horse, whose rider is called Faithful and True. With justice he judges and wages war. His eyes are like blazing fire, and on his head are many crowns. He has a name written on him that no one knows but he himself. He is dressed in a robe dipped in blood, and his name is the Word of God. The armies of heaven were following him, riding on white horses and dressed in fine linen, white and clean. Coming out of his mouth is a sharp sword with which to strike down the nations. "He will rule them with an iron scepter."*

Psalm 96:12–13 Questions

Why will the fields be jubilant and the trees in the forest sing for joy?

Read John 5:27–30. By whose authority is Jesus sent to judge the world?

Does the world deserve judgement? If so, why?

Read 1 Thessalonians 1:10. How did God prove that Jesus was His son and qualified to judge the world in perfect righteousness?

PSALM 109:4–5

In return for my friendship they accuse me, but I am a man of prayer. They repay me evil for good, and hatred for my friendship.

Please read the reference verses and the fulfillment verse below, then answer the questions on the next page.

REFERENCES

Psalm 69:13: *But I pray to you, LORD, in the time of your favor; in your great love, O God, answer me with your sure salvation.*

Matthew 5:43–45: *You have heard that it was said, "Love your neighbor and hate your enemy." But I tell you, love your enemies and pray for those who persecute you, that you may be children of your Father in heaven. He causes his sun to rise on the evil and the good, and sends rain on the righteous and the unrighteous."*

Romans 12:20: *On the contrary: "If your enemy is hungry, feed him; if he is thirsty, give him something to drink. In doing this, you will heap burning coals on his head."*

Proverbs 25:21–22: *If your enemy is hungry, give him food to eat; if he is thirsty, give him water to drink. In doing this, you will heap burning coals on his head, and the LORD will reward you.*

FULFILLMENT

Luke 23:34: *Jesus said, "Father, forgive them, for they do not know what they are doing."*

Psalm 109:4–5 Questions

Have you ever been betrayed by a close friend? If yes, can you explain?

Have you ever been betrayed by someone you were trying to help?

Unlike Jesus, you were probably surprised, weren't you?

How did you react?

Do you think Jesus ever treated Judas different from the other disciples?

What does Jesus' treatment of Judas reveal to you about His character?

Read Matthew 5:43–45. In your own words, what do these verses ask us to do for our friends and enemies?

It has become kind of a cliche now, but the question, "What Would Jesus Do?" is very appropriate and easy to answer in most circumstances. Would you agree?

PSALM 109:8

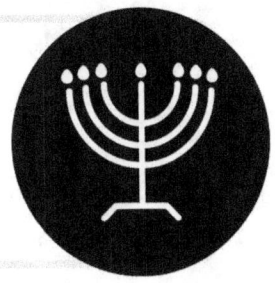

May his days be few; may another take his place of leadership.

Please read the reference verse and the fulfillment verse below, then answer the questions on the following page.

REFERENCE

Psalm 69:25: *May their place be deserted; let there be no one to dwell in their tents.*

FULFILLMENT

Acts 1:20–26: *"For," said Peter, "it is written in the Book of Psalms: 'May his place be deserted; let there be no one to dwell in it,' and, 'May another take his place of leadership.' Therefore it is necessary to choose one of the men who have been with us the whole time the Lord Jesus went in and out among us, beginning from John's baptism to the time when Jesus was taken up from us. For one of these must become a witness with us of his resurrection." So they nominated two men: Joseph called Barsabbas (also known as Justus) and Mathias. Then they prayed, "Lord, you know everyone's heart. Show us which of these two you have chosen to take over this apostolic ministry, which Judas left to go where he belongs." Then they cast lots, and the lot fell to Mathias; so he was added to the eleven apostles.**

---

* The first time anyone prayed to Jesus. The last time anyone cast lots.

Psalm 109:8 Questions

In our fulfillment verses, Acts: 1:20–26, the apostles went about the selection process in a very specific way. Most importantly, they asked for God's guidance first.

When making important decisions for you or your family, do you generally follow these same guidelines? Do you follow them in your workplace? Is there a difference in when you pray if it's a trivial decision or an important one?

Does your church routinely ask for guidance from God, or do they skip that part of the process?

Do the leaders in your life tend to get ahead of God and then try to be patient while He catches up? Or do they carefully go to God in prayer and then wait to hear His voice before acting?

LESSON 8

PSALM 110:1

*The LORD says to my Lord: "Sit at my right hand
until I make your enemies a footstool for your feet."*

Please read the reference verses and fulfillment verses below, then answer the questions on the following page.

REFERENCES

Mark 12:36: *David himself, speaking by the Holy Spirit, declared: "The Lord said to my Lord: 'Sit at my right hand until I put your enemies under your feet.'"*

Acts 2:34–35: *For David did not ascend to heaven, and yet he said, "The Lord said to my Lord: 'Sit at my right hand until I make your enemies a footstool for your feet.'"*

FULFILLMENT

Matthew 22:41–46: *While the Pharisees were gathered together, Jesus asked them, "What do you think about the Messiah? Whose son is he?" "The son of David," they replied. He said to them, "How is it then that David, speaking by the Spirit, calls him 'Lord'? For he says, 'The Lord said to my Lord: "Sit at my right hand until I put your enemies under your feet." If then David calls him 'Lord,' how can he be his son?" No one could say a word in reply, and from that day on no one dared to ask him any more questions.*

Hebrews 10:11–14: *Day after day every priest stands and performs his religious duties; again and again he offers the same sacrifices, which can never take away sins. But when this priest had offered for all time one sacrifice for sins, he sat down at the right hand of God, and since that time he waits for his enemies to be made his footstool. For by one sacrifice he has made perfect forever those who are being made holy.*

Psalm 110:1 Questions

Read Matthew 22:42 (part of our fulfillment verse). It is possibly the most important question we can ask ourselves:

"What do you believe about Christ?"

Whose Son is Christ?

Can you cite some Scripture that proves how you feel?

Did the Pharisees know that the Messiah would be a descendant of David?

List Scripture references to show that the Pharisees either knew or did not know that the Messiah would be a descendant of David.

PSALM 110:4

The Lord has sworn and will not change his mind:
"You are a priest forever, in the order of Melchizedek."

Please read the reference verses and the fulfillment verses, then answer the questions on the following page.

REFERENCES

Numbers 23:19: *God is not human, that he should lie, not a human being, that he should change his mind. Does he speak and then not act? Does he promise and not fulfill?*

Hebrews 7:20–22: *And it was not without an oath! Others became priests without any oath, but he became a priest with an oath when God said to him: "The Lord has sworn and will not change his mind: 'You are a priest forever.'" Because of this oath, Jesus has become the guarantor of a better covenant.*

FULFILLMENTS

Hebrews 6:20: *Where our forerunner, Jesus, has entered on our behalf. He has become a high priest forever, in the order of Melchizedek.*

Hebrews 10:11–12: *Day after day every priest stands and performs his religious duties; again and again he offers the same sacrifices, which can never take away sins. But when this priest had offered for all time one sacrifice for sins, he sat down at the right hand of God.*

Psalm 110:4 Questions

Duties of the high priest included being in charge of all other priests. He was the only one who could go into the Most Holy Place, and then only once a year on the Day of Atonement to atone for the sins of the whole nation.

Jesus is always in the Most Holy Place with the Father.

Read Genesis 14:17:20.

What does Melchizedek mean?

What does King of Salem mean?

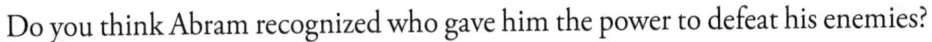

Do you think Abram recognized who gave him the power to defeat his enemies?

Who gave him that power?

Read Genesis 14:18–20.

God clearly spoke through Melchizedek. Do you listen to God and let Him speak through you? Can you give a personal example of when you listened to God?

Read Hebrews 4:14. Why is Jesus a greater high priest than any other?

PSALM 118:22

The stone the builders rejected has become the cornerstone.

Please read the reference verses and the fulfillment verse below, then answer the questions on the following page.

REFERENCES

Matthew 21:42–44: *Jesus said to them, "Have you never read in the Scriptures: 'The stone the builders rejected has become the cornerstone; the Lord has done this, and it is marvelous in our eyes'? Therefore I tell you that the kingdom of God will be taken away from you and given to a people who will produce its fruit. Anyone who falls on this stone will be broken to pieces, anyone on whom it falls will be crushed."*

Acts 4:11–12: *Jesus is "'the stone you builders rejected, which has become the cornerstone.' Salvation is found in no one else, for there is no other name under heaven given to mankind by which we must be saved."*

FULFILLMENT

1 Peter 2:4–8: *As you come to him, the living Stone—rejected by humans but chosen by God and precious to him—you also, like living stones, are being built*

into a spiritual house to be a holy priesthood, offering spiritual sacrifices acceptable to God through Jesus Christ. For in Scripture it says: "See, I lay a stone in Zion, a chosen and precious cornerstone, and the one who trusts in him will never be put to shame." Now to you who believe, this stone is precious. But to those who do not believe, "The stone the builders rejected has become the cornerstone," and "A stone that causes people to stumble and a rock that makes them fall." They stumble because they disobey the message—which is also what they were destined for.

Psalm 118:22 Questions

Read Matthew 21:42–44.

What does "on whom it falls will be crushed" mean to you?

Look up the definition of *cornerstone*.

In our fulfillment verses, 1 Peter 2:4–8, why do you think men continue to stumble?

PSALM 118:26

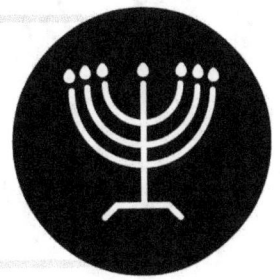

Blessed is he who comes in the name of the LORD.
From the house of the LORD we bless you.

Please read the reference and fulfillment verses below, then answer the questions on the following page.

REFERENCES

Luke 13:35: *Look, your house is left to you desolate. I tell you, you will not see me again until you say, "Blessed is he who comes in the name of the Lord."*

Luke 19:38: *Blessed is the king who comes in the name of the Lord! Peace in heaven and glory in the highest!*

FULFILLMENT

Matthew 21:9: *The crowds that went ahead of him and those that followed shouted, "Hosanna to the Son of David!" "Blessed is he who comes in the name of the Lord!" "Hosanna in the highest heaven!"*

Psalm 118:26 Questions

What does "Hosanna" mean?

Do you think the people wanted a savior at this point, or did they even realize they needed one?

Or, were the people looking for a conquering hero?

If they were searching for a conquering hero, why?

How long before this crowd who was praising Jesus would turn completely against Him and literally want His blood?

Many people in the crowd wanting Jesus crucified would have seen some of His miracles. What happened to change their hearts? Was it purely an emotional response? Were they carried away by the crowds? How do you think things changed so quickly?

PSALM 130:7–8

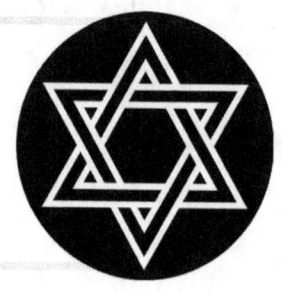

O Israel, put your hope in the LORD, for with the LORD is unfailing love and with him is full redemption. He himself will redeem Israel from all their sins.

Please read the reference verses and the fulfillment verse below, then answer the questions on the following page.

REFERENCES

Psalm 111:9: *He provided redemption for his people; he ordained his covenant forever—holy and awesome is his name.*

Luke 7:14–15:* *Then he went up and touched the bier they were carrying him on, and the bearers stood still. He said, "Young man, I say to you, get up!" The dead man sat up and began to talk, and Jesus gave him back to his mother.*

---

* Salvation, we are all dead in our sin. Jesus gives us back our life. The dead man did not earn his second chance at life, and neither do we.

FULFILLMENT

Luke 1:68:** *Praise be to the Lord, the God of Israel, because he has come to his people and redeemed them.*

** Zechariah praised God with the first words he was able to speak in months. The Messiah was coming in his lifetime, and his own son would pave the way for him.

Psalm 130:7–8 Questions

Read Luke 7:14–15.

Did the dead man earn his second chance at life?

Read our fulfillment verse, Luke 1:68.

Who was talking?

Who was he talking about?

Do you give God praise first?

Jesus the Messiah was coming in his lifetime, and his own Son would pave the way for him.

ABOUT THE AUTHOR

The author of this Bible study workbook is not the one sitting down to type this page. The Author of this workbook is the Author of all creation. I am simply the scribe who was given the gift of this project by almighty God, writing everything our Lord required of me from start to finish, and faithfully copying all Scripture from His Holy Bible.

Within about twenty-four hours of my salvation on March 30, 2006, the Lord instilled in me a voracious appetite for reading His Word. He led my husband and me to open a Christian bookstore in Estes Park, Colorado, in June of that same year. Throughout that process for the next three years, God put amazing Christians in my life to teach and guide me, indwelling me with the Holy Spirit to explain things I did not understand so that I could pass those things on to other people.

I happily belong to Cornerstone Baptist Church in Estes Park. My husband and I have been active members of Gideons International for the last sixteen years and have been extremely blessed by the people we have met through the organization and the people we have been able to serve.

I have been very blessed to be allowed to live in this beautiful mountain community for over thirty-seven years now with my husband, John, two dogs, Esther and Ezekiel, and two cats, Samson and Delilah, who keep me laughing all day long.

APPENDIX

See Scripture references below for further reading about the parallels existing between David and Jesus.

- David was from Bethlehem. He was a shepherd in the Bethlehem Valley where sacrificial lambs were raised. Jesus was the Lamb, the Good Shepherd.

- 1 Samuel 17:1–58 David's family didn't believe in him and repeatedly discouraged him, as did Jesus' family. See Psalm 69.

- Jesse (David's Father) means "man." Both David and Jesus are referred to as the "Son of Man"

- Five loaves of bread for David's starving men in 1 Samuel 21:3 (consecrated). Jesus feeds the five thousand with five loaves of bread in Mark 6:41.

- Both men were always on the move. David was running from Saul. In Matthew 8:20, Jesus replied, *"Foxes have dens and birds have nests, but the Son of Man has no place to lay his head."*

- David was thirty years old when he became king. Jesus began his ministry when he was thirty years old.

- Both had enemies without cause. David's men betrayed him and went with Absalom. Jesus had the Pharisees and Sadducees, who should have believed in Him. (Psalm 35).

- Both were betrayed by a close friend. David was betrayed by Ahithopel. Jesus was betrayed by Judas Iscariot (Psalm 41).

- In 1 Chronicles 17:16 King David humbled himself and sat before the LORD. The only person in the Bible to ever do that. Of course Jesus always sits at the right hand of the Father.

DELEGATING RESPONSIBILITY

- David: 2 Samuel 8:16–18—David appoints his officials.
- Jesus: Matthew 4:19—Jesus is making His disciples fishers of men.
- Matthew 10:1—Jesus sent out the twelve.
- Luke 10:1–23—Jesus sends out the seventy-two.
- Revelation 5:10, 20:6—Priests of God and Christ will reign with him one thousand years.

HUMBLE

- David: 2 Samuel 7:1–2
- David: 2 Samuel 7:18–21
- Jesus: Luke 22:26–27—Jesus serves.
- Jesus: John 13:1–7—Jesus washes the disciples' feet.

SYMPATHETIC

- David: 2 Samuel 9:1–12
- Jesus: Mark 9:21–27

There are many "parallel" headings courtesy of Beth Moore's Bible study: "David Seeking a Heart Like His."

ACCOUNTABLE (means responsible, answerable)

- David was totally accountable to God for everything. See 2 Samuel 7:18 where he asks of God what he could do for him?
- John 4:34: *"My food," said Jesus, "is to do the will of him who sent me and to finish his work."*
- John 7:16: *Jesus answered, "My teaching is not my own. It comes from the one who sent me."*
- John 5:19: *Jesus gave them this answer: "Very truly I tell you, the Son can do nothing by himself."*
- Luke 9:12–17: Jesus feeds the five thousand that are following him.

HEART FOR WORSHIP

- David: 2 Samuel 6:12–16—Bringing the ark of the covenant to Jerusalem.
- Jesus: Hebrews 2:11: *Both the one who makes men holy and those who are made holy are of the same family.*

TOTAL COOPERATION WITH GOD

- David: 1 Samuel 16:23: Whenever the spirit from God came upon Saul, David would take up his harp and play.
- 1 Samuel 18:12–14: Saul was afraid of David because the Lord was with David but had left Saul.
- 1 Samuel 24:5: *Afterward, David was conscious, stricken for having cut off a corner of his robe.*
- 1 Samuel 24:9: *He said to Saul, "Why do you listen when men say, 'David is bent on harming you'?*
- 1 Samuel 26:11: *But The Lord forbid that I should lay a hand on the Lord's anointed. Now get the spear and water jug that are near his head, and let's go.*
- Jesus: John 5:19: *Jesus gave them this answer: "Very truly I tell you, the Son can do nothing by himself; he can do only what he sees his Father doing, because whatever the Father does the Son also does."*
- John 7:16: *Jesus answered, "My teaching is not my own. It comes from the one who sent me."*
- John 8:16: *But if I do judge, my decisions are true, because I am not alone. I stand with the Father, who sent me*

DEDICATED EVERY TREASURE TO GOD

- David: 2 Samuel 8:1–12. In verses 11–12, *King David dedicated these articles to the Lord, as he had done with the silver and gold from all the nations he had subdued.*
- Jesus: John 17:9–12: Jesus dedicated all of the people of the world (his greatest treasure) to God: *"All I have is yours, and all you have is mine."*

COMPASSION

- David: 2 Samuel 9:1: *David asked, "Is there anyone still left of the house of Saul to whom I can show kindness for Jonathan's sake?"*
- 2 Samuel 10:5: *When David was told about this, he sent messengers to meet the men, for they were greatly humiliated.*
- Jesus throughout the gospels:
    - *Mark 8:1–3: "I have compassion." Jesus feeds the four thousand.*
    - *John 4:7–26: the Samaritan Woman at the well*
    - *John 8:1–11: the woman the Pharisees wanted to stone*

Notes About David

ew biblical characters are more compelling to read and learn about than
David. As we all know, when we first heard of him (1 Samuel 16–17) he
was a boy and a shepherd, a confident hunter of lions and bears, the anointed
one of God. He was a giant killer, a musician, and a composer. He was the King
of Israel, an adulterer, a murderer, and a man after Gods own heart. However,
many of us missed that he was not just "Israel's singer of songs" (2 Samuel
23:1) but also a prophet. In Psalm 2, David describes a rebellion in the nations
against the Anointed one. Psalm 16 is just one of many of his "songs." In Psalm
16, he was not talking about himself, but the Messiah's body not seeing decay.

Of the twenty-four Messianic Psalms we discuss in this study, we know
that David wrote at least sixteen of them. Please keep in mind throughout the
study that David wrote these Psalms one thousand years before the birth of
Messiah.

In 2 Kings 8:16–19, it details the fifth year of Joram son of Ahab king of
Israel, when Jehoshaphat was king of Judah, Jehoram son of Jehoshaphat began
his reign as king of Judah. He was thirty-two years old when he became king,
and he reigned in Jerusalem eight years. He walked in the ways of the kings of
Israel, as the house of Ahab had done, for he married a daughter of Ahab. He
did evil in the eyes of the Lord. Nevertheless, for the sake of his servant David,
the Lord was not willing to destroy Judah. He had promised to maintain a
lamp for David and his descendants forever.

I am very happy and blessed to be able to share this small part of David's
life with you as it relates to the coming Messiah.

Following is a list of prophetic Psalms specific to Jesus' suffering and
crucifixion:

- Psalm 22:1
- Psalm 22:7–8
- Psalm 22:15
- Psalm 22:16
- Psalm 22:18
- Psalm 31:5
- Psalm 34:19–20
- Psalm 35:11
- Psalm 38:11
- Psalm 41:9
- Psalm 55:12–14
- Psalm 69:9
- Psalm 69:21*

---

* Further reading: Matthew Henry's commentary on Psalm 69:21: "See how particularly the sufferings of Christ were foretold, which proves the Scripture to be the Word of God, and how exactly the predictions were fulfilled in Jesus Christ, which proves Him to be the true Messiah. This is He who should come, and we are to look for no other."

Synopsis of David's Psalms

In Psalm 2, David described a rebellion of the nations against the Anointed One, Messiah, and His eternal reign.

In Psalm 8, David wrote about Messiah being ruler over everything: flocks, herds, birds of the air, and fish of the sea.

In Psalm 16, David was not talking about himself, but Messiah's body not seeing decay.

In Psalm 22, David prophesied about many of the things that Jesus would encounter on His road to Calvary, plus many things He would speak from the cross.

In Psalm 31, David spoke words that Jesus would speak from the cross.

David wrote Psalm 34 while pretending to be insane in front of Abimelech. In this Psalm he wrote, *"He protects all his bones, not one of them will be broken"* (v. 20).

In Psalm 35, David wrote about having enemies without cause (perhaps those who followed Absalom?) and those who hated him without reason. Jesus also had many enemies without cause.

In Psalm 38, David wrote about companions and friends who avoided him.

In Psalm 40, David spoke of an experience that Jesus would have in the synagogue.

In Psalm 41, David wrote about the pain of being betrayed by a close friend. In his case, it was Ahithophel.

In Psalm 55, David once again explained about the pain of being betrayed by a close companion.

In Psalm 68, David wrote about the Savior ascending on high and leading his captives from sin and Satan as if it had already happened.

In Psalm 69, David again wrote of his experiences and paralleled his life to Jesus' life: *"I am foreigner to my own family, a stranger to my own mother's children"* (v. 8).

Psalm 72 is primarily a Messianic Psalm written by David, possibly on his death bed. It is about Jesus' birth and a tribute from kings. How His life on earth was spent defending and delivering the needy and afflicted. His name will endure as long as the sun. He will rule to the ends of the earth. All nations will be blessed through Him (vv. 4–5, 11).

In Psalm 109, David wrote about betrayal, the pain of being repaid evil for good, and having to replace a leader.

In Psalm 110, David spoke of his enemies being made a footstool, as will Jesus' enemies. Then he spoke of the eternal Priest King (vv. 1, 4).